STARTINGUP NOW

24 Steps To Launch Your Own Business

L. Brian Jenkins, M.A.

Foreword by: Don G. Soderquist

Vice Chairman & COO, Walmart Stores, Inc.

STARTINGUP NOW

ACCLAIM FOR STARTINGUP NOW

"StartingUp is a complete guide for novice and experienced entrepreneurs who know that today they cannot afford to make time-consuming and expensive mistakes, and who are committed to maximizing their chances for success. The guide provides a holistic system of dealing with personal growth issues that are so important for business leaders to deal with, as well as developing key business concepts, and wrapping it around technology that progressive entrepreneurs must be able to navigate."

—Dr. Zira J. Smith, Entrepreneurship & Small Business Educator
University of Illinois-Cook County

"I think you have indeed put together the fundamental steps that a person needs to take in developing a successful business—based on my own experience."

—Dr. Melvin Banks Sr., Founder, Urban Ministries, Inc.

"StartingUp is a new and exciting tool for entrepreneurs of all ages. If you are just starting your business or are a seasoned business owner needing quick answers and easy access, StartingUp is for you. I highly recommend this revolutionary tool."

—Andre Thornton, President & CEO, ASW Global, LLC

STARTINGUP NOW

ACCLAIM FOR STARTINGUP NOW

"No more excuses! StartingUp Now is your blue print for business creation that will become a lasting resource to turn your idea into your future."

—Jeffrey Weber, Entrepreneur & Author of IDEA to Exit

"The StartingUp Skill Center lets me interact with other students who own their business. We share ideas, links, and tips online. I've met people, other kids actually, interested in owning their own business from around the world."

—William, High School Student Business Owner

"StartingUp Now has several useful and beneficial applications. As a business owner for many years and an entrepreneurship education proponent, I highly recommend StartingUp Now as an excellent resource for both those new to business and those who instruct individuals in principles of entrepreneurship. The website is easy to navigate and provides excellent answers to many frequently asked questions relative to business structure. I've read many books on business development and this resource is one of the best new books on the market. As a pastor, I feel this tool will be useful as our board of leaders embark on strategic planning for the ministry."

—Dr. Hazel A. King, President, H.A. King & Associates, Inc.
Pastor, Greater Faith Ministries International

...continued

ACCLAIM FOR STARTINGUP NOW

"StartingUp Now takes a fresh and modern approach to planning the launch of a business. The bite-size chunks of information, flexible format, and mobile access make this guide more relevant and useful for today's entrepreneurs."

—Raman Chadha, Executive Director & Clinical Professor
DePaul University, Coleman Entrepreneurship Center

"StartingUp Now has helped me tremendously not just as an entrepreneur, but as an individual that believes in destiny and manifestation of ideas through one's individual talents and beliefs. The great thing about entrepreneurship is the idea of creating nothing from something. Entrepreneurship leaves me with no excuses—just limitless opportunities. And StartingUp Now helps all believers in greatness make their dreams a reality."

—Stephan Hall, Entrenuity Alum, Partner
Trash Geeks, Inc.

STARTINGUP NOW

ACCLAIM FOR STARTINGUP NOW

"Brian has been on the front lines of innovative youth work for almost two decades. StartingUp Now is his life passion to provide practical, real, transferrable principles and skills to train youth and adults to OWN their business."

—Phil Jackson, Pastor & Founder of The House Covenant Church
Author: The Hip Hop Church

"Entrepreneurship is a language that needs to be spoken by people everywhere. The StartingUp Now toolkit is an accessible and much-needed on ramp to the world of value creation and self-sustainability."

—Rodolpho Carrasco, U.S. Regional Facilitator,
Partners Worldwide and
Director, Two Forty Group

Published in the United States by StartingUp Business Solutions, Chicago, Illinois
www.startingupnow.com

ISBN-13: 978-0615457710
ISBN-10: 0615457711

Printed in the United States of America

Design by: Kathyjo Varco, Big Sound Music, Inc.
Edited by: Vicki D. Frye, Fryeday Everyday

10 9 8 7 6 5 4 3 2 1

First Edition

DEDICATION

Thank you, Jenai Jenkins—my wife, life-partner, a model mother to my children, and friend. Without your unequivocal support, the experiences learned and shared in this book would not be possible. You are the woman so eloquently defined by Solomon in Proverbs 31:10–31. I also dedicate this book to our children—Bria Nichelle, Lawrence Braxton, and Brooke Elise—who inspire me daily to strive to be the best father I know how to be. I'm still working on it...

To my parents, Larry and Madelyn Jenkins—you define what it means to support and guide your children. Thank you for always being there.

TABLE OF CONTENTS

STARTINGUP NOW

STARTINGUP KEY GUIDE

Get familiar with what's inside. Use this overview to navigate through each StartingUp Key Lesson. Take advantage of the space on the right of each lesson for notes and answering questions.

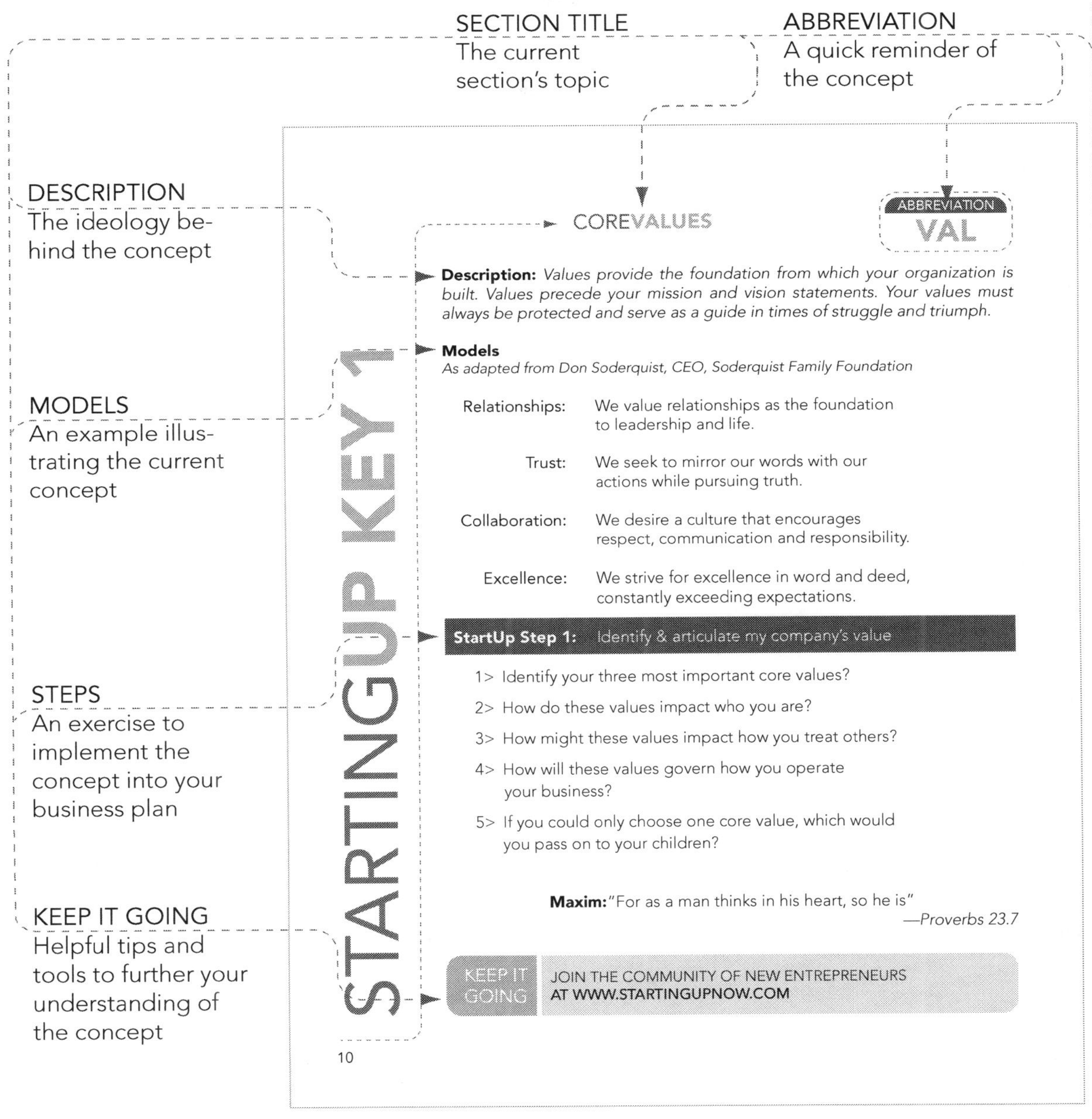

FOREWORD

Entrepreneurship is what has driven the free enterprise system in our country since our founding fathers established the foundation for our way of life. Brian Jenkins is an entrepreneur by heart and by experience. I have known him for almost 10 years. During that time I have been impressed with his passion for entrepreneurship. I have witnessed his ability to create and build his own business based on a clear understanding of what it takes to start a business founded on vision, mission, and values with limited resources. His ability to "stick with it" in difficult circumstances and maintain his commitment is precisely the type of leadership entrepreneurs and business owners need to see in today's economically challenged marketplace.

Brian has demonstrated a passion for training youth, educators, business owners, and the formerly incarcerated in free market principles. I believe that Brian has the personal experience, integrity, training skills, and know-how to impact business owners for years to come.

When ambitious individuals have an idea that they believe has merit as a product or service, it is difficult to find a road map that helps them get started and carry through to completion. Brian has framed StartingUp Now in such a way that it provides a time-tested, step-by-step process to achieve success. I believe that StartingUp Now will have a significant impact on all who read it.

—Donald G. Soderquist, ret.,
Vice Chairman and Chief Operating Officer
Walmart Stores, Inc.

INTRODUCTION

StartingUp Now is a practical, easy-to-understand business-planning guide for the new entrepreneur with great ideas and limited business planning knowledge, who needs steps to get started. *StartingUp Now* employs elements of today's texting culture to quickly communicate essential business principles. Each *StartingUp Key* leads the future entrepreneur through a memorable abbreviation, informative definition, useful examples, and constructive prompts in a journal-style format that ultimately provides users with the opportunity to formulate their business plans.

Upon formulating your plan with the StartingUp Business Plan Template, log in to your customized profile page on the StartingUp Now Skill Center (SUSC) and enter your business plan information on the online template. For those with mobile devices, you can access your business plan and other tools and resources on the go.

Welcome to *StartingUp Now!*

STARTINGUP NOW

CORE VALUES

Description: *Values provide the foundation from which your organization is built. Values precede your mission and vision statements. Your values must always be protected and serve as a guide in times of struggle and triumph.*

Models

As adapted from Don Soderquist, CEO, Soderquist Family Foundation

Relationships:	We value relationships as the foundation to leadership and life.
Trust:	We seek to mirror our words with our actions while pursuing truth.
Collaboration:	We desire a culture that encourages respect, communication, and responsibility.
Excellence:	We strive for excellence in word and deed, constantly exceeding expectations.

StartUp Step 1: Identify & articulate my company's values.

1> Identify your three most important core values.

2> How do these values impact who you are?

3> How might these values impact how you treat others?

4> How will these values govern how you operate your business?

5> If you could only choose one core value, which would you pass on to your children?

Maxim: "For as a man thinks in his heart, so is he."
—***Proverbs 23:7, New King James Version***

KEEP IT GOING — JOIN THE COMMUNITY OF NEW ENTREPRENEURS AT WWW.STARTINGUPNOW.COM.

MISSIONSTATEMENT

Description: *The MST provides purpose. It defines what you want the business to become; not necessarily its current status. The MST should be challenging but also achievable.*

Models

"To equip youth workers with the expertise necessary to train young people to be skillful entrepreneurs with integrity."

—Entrenuity, NFP

"Our mission revolves around one word: patience. In earnest pursuit of excellent performance and outstanding client service, **patience** is our over-arching virtue. By taking a long-term view, we are able to build our firm around these core values: focus, independent thinking, and teamwork."

—Ariel Capital Investments, Inc.

StartUp Step 2: Establish my company's MST.

1> Why am I starting the business? What are the motivating factors?

2> What is the company's purpose?

3> What do I hope the company will accomplish?

4> What product does my company sell or what service does it provide?

5> How is my company different?

Maxim: "Purpose is what gives life meaning."
—Charles H. Perkhurst

KEEP IT GOING

GET ON-GOING SUPPORT FOR YOUR NEW VENTURE AT WWW.STARTINGUPNOW.COM.

MYMST

VISIONSTATEMENT

Description: *The VIS is the idealistic objective that stretches an organization beyond its current status and declares its future purpose. It is the level of excellence or accomplishment that the business is motivated to achieve. The VIS represents the "best."*

Models

"To see young people around the globe receive hands-on entrepreneurship training that develops skills and values to be leaders in their chosen marketplace, community, and family."

—Entrenuity, NFP

"To bring inspiration and innovation to every athlete in the world."

—Nike

"McDonald's vision is to be the world's best quick service restaurant experience. Being the best means providing outstanding quality, service, cleanliness, and value, so that we make every customer in every restaurant smile."

—McDonald's, Inc.

StartUp Step 3: To cast a vision for your business, let's start by doing the following:

1> Five years from now your business is receiving the Small Business of the Year Award. In what categories would the business receive nominations (leadership, green technology, innovation, etc.)?

2> What are the accomplished goals that you can look back on?

3> What impact has your business made on your community or industry?

4> What do you want to be known for?

Next, condense your findings from each of the four numbered sections into a single sentence statement.

KEEP IT GOING — FOR HELP TO MAKE YOUR VISION A REALITY, LOG ON TO WWW.STARTINGUPNOW.COM.

Now, take the sentences and reduce them to a short statement that you can almost memorize.

If your statement totals three sentences or fewer, you're done! If not, summarize your statement into three sentences or fewer and verbally share it with someone in 30 seconds or fewer. If it takes longer, you have more work to do!

Maxim: "Desire is the starting point of all achievement, not a hope, not a wish, but a keen pulsating desire which transcends everything."
—Napoleon Hill

MYVIS

EXECUTIVE SUMMARY

Description: *The EXE describes the company, the product/service being sold, and the uniqueness of the investment opportunity. Potential financiers will focus first on the EXE; based on this, they will then decide whether or not to examine the viability of the business for investment.*

Models

Pet Daycare Executive Summary:

Pet Daycare offers on-site pet-sitting services for dogs and cats, providing the personal loving pet care that the owners themselves would provide if they were there. While there are currently eight businesses offering pet-sitting in Oak Park, only four of these offer on-site pet care and none offers "pet visit" services for working pet owners. Based on the size of our market and our defined market area, our sales projections for the first year are $340,000. We are seeking an operating line of $150,000 to finance our first year growth. Together, the co-owners have invested $62,000 to meet working capital requirements.

Wendy's Franchise Executive Summary:

Wendy's International, Inc., and its subsidiaries engage in the operation, development, and franchising of a range of quick service, casual restaurants. Wendy's International, Inc., is one of the world's largest restaurant operating and franchising companies with $11.6 billion in system-wide sales and more than 9,700 total restaurants. The company's quality brands are Wendy's Old Fashioned Hamburgers, Tim Hortons, and Baja Fresh Mexican Grill. The company invested in two additional quality brands during 2002: Cafe Express and Pasta Pomodoro. Wendy's International, Inc., was founded in 1969 by Dave Thomas and is based in Dublin, Ohio. This offering represents an excellent opportunity for an investor to purchase an absolute triple net leased, free-standing Wendy's with an outstanding operator of 20 Wendy's restaurants in Chicago, who is consistently in the top 10% operators in the nation. This approximately 3,000+/- square-foot, freestanding Wendy's property generates $136,000 annually, is on a brand new 20-year absolute lease, with 10% rental escalations every fifth year.

KEEP IT GOING

JOIN THE COMMUNITY OF NEW ENTREPRENEURS AT WWW.STARTINGUPNOW.COM.

StartUp Step 4: Use the following steps to create your Executive Summary. Don't panic and plan for many edits. In most cases, the EXE changes multiple times and is not final until you complete the business plan.

1> Describe the product or service you are selling.

2> List out the unique features and describe how they directly benefit the customer.

3> What makes this investment opportunity unique?

Maxim: "Give me six hours to chop down a tree and I'll spend the first hour sharpening the ax."
—Abraham Lincoln, 16th President of the United States of America.

MYEXE

ELEVATOR SPEECH

Description: *A brief yet persuasive description of what you do, the product you produce, and the service you provide. The ESP will summarize your business expertise in the time it might take for an elevator to journey from the ground floor to the penthouse.*

Models

"I turn conflict into agreement. I'm Robbie Smith of the Business Conflict Resolution Center. My workshops & coaching reduce your conflict. We teach people how to understand, discuss, and resolve conflict so they can live happier lives. Let US replace the conflict in your life."

—*Business Conflict Resolution Center, LLC.*

"Hello, I teach college graduates manners and business etiquette for interviews. Politeness promotes profits in the interview process. I'm Jasmine Jones, and it's my pleasure to meet you!"

"I'm Walter Smith of Romantic Meals. I specialize in providing immaculate 5-star meals for anniversaries, birthdays, or special occasions at your home. We provide the meal so you can provide the mood!"

—*Romantic Meals, LLC.*

StartUp Step 5: Your ESP should be very clear, descriptive, and to the point.

Tips for your ESP:

1> Make it easy to understand.

2> Make it brief, precise, and to the point.

3> Leave no questions that need to be answered.

4> Practice it verbally. Try to say your ESP in 60 seconds or less.

Maxim: KIS Method—Keep It Simple

KEEP IT GOING — SHARPEN YOUR ENTREPRENEURIAL SKILLS AT WWW.STARTINGUPNOW.COM.

BIOGRAPHY

Description: *Everyone has a story. Tell yours. Your BIO is the personal story of how you got started, your motivation, your skills, and your goals. Make this personal.*

Samples

"In the sixth grade my parents forced me to attend an entrepreneurship program at my school. My friend and I were the youngest in the class. I was nervous, scared, and really wanted to play on the basketball team instead of being in the class. The class taught us a lot about business. We identified a market need (vending), created a business plan, and opened for business. The business was very prosperous over the next two years. We made over $10,000 annually. We were introduced to investing and wanted to grow to the next phase. Upon going to high school, I started additional businesses and was fascinated by the stock market and wanted to learn more. I completed a 2-year internship program with a large investment firm in New York, and now I'm a First Year Investor with that same investment firm in NYC. It all started with that entrepreneurship class; it taught me "anything is possible."

—Stephan Hall, First Year Investor, Goldman Sachs

StartUp Step 6: Writing your personal story can be both challenging and revealing. Let the following questions prompt you. Go ahead…get started.

THIS IS YOUR STORY

1> My name is ________________ and I'm from ________________.

2> My journey started when…

3> This happened in __________ (year) of when I was ____________.

4> Why do I continue? I believe it's for the reason of ______________.

5> My words of wisdom are….

Maxim: "What would you attempt to do if you knew you would not fail."
—Author Unknown

KEEP IT GOING: FIND BIO EXAMPLES FROM OTHER ENTREPRENEURS AT WWW.STARTINGUPNOW.COM.

MYBIO

THE BIG IDEA

Description: *Coming up with a great business idea doesn't need to be complicated. Combine a NEED with something you love to do, then create your business.*

Models

"People enjoy eating ice cream, so why shouldn't dogs enjoy ice cream, too? Sounds crazy to some, but the lack of frozen treats for my dogs gave me this bright and unique idea."

—*Chellsy Charles, Owner, Chilly-Dawgs*

"Store brands of lotions irritate my skin. After trying prescriptions from doctors and home remedies, I learned how to make my own lotion using natural products. Now I sell it for others just like me."

—*Kim Porter, Founder, LeNae Natural Lotions*

"My grandmother is especially important to me and she still enjoys looking her best. Although she lacks the mobility she used to have, she still enjoys her day at the spa. I now provide home based facials, manicures, and pedicures for seniors at their homes."

—*Julia Smiley, CEO, Mobile Spas, LLC.*

StartUp Step 7: Generating Ideas

Businesses typically invent a new product or service to fulfill a need or improve an existing product or service already in the marketplace. Oftentimes entrepreneurs will center their interests, experiences, passions, and skill sets toward their business ideas. To put it simply, Do What You Love.

1> Make a list of your hobbies, interests, or talents. Which of these would you do whether you got paid for it or not?

2> Narrow this list to your top three choices.

3> Which of these things could satisfy a marketplace need? Is that need currently being met? If so, how and by whom? Can it be improved?

4> How can you make this idea uniquely yours?

KEEP IT GOING — SHARE YOUR BUSINESS IDEAS AND EXPLORE OTHERS AT WWW.STARTINGUPNOW.COM.

Maxim: "Find a job you love and you'll never work a day in your life."
—Confucius

MYIDEA

LEGAL STRUCTURE

Description: *Legal structures are designed for the protection of the business owner and its customers. There are several types of legal structures and which one is best depends on your personal and business needs.*

Models

Most entrepreneurs select one of the following legal structures for their businesses. While you should educate yourself by conducting your own research, it is also wise to consult an attorney or legal expert to review your selection and confirm that you've chosen the legal structure that will best serve your business now and in the future.

Sole Proprietorship means one owner who assumes all risk and receives all the rewards. Typically, they are less expensive to form and operate.

Partnerships are a legal structure in which the partners (owners) share the profits and losses of the business. Partnerships are generally not taxed on profits prior to the profits being distributed to the owners.

Limited Liability Corporations (LLC) is a flexible legal structure that blends aspects of both a partnership and corporation. The primary characteristic an LLC shares with a corporation is limited liability, and the primary characteristic it shares with a partnership is the availability of pass-through income taxation. It is often more flexible than a corporation and well suited for companies with a single owner.

C Corporations can have an unlimited number of owners. They are publicly traded, meaning individuals, other corporations, partnerships, and the general public can purchase shares of stock in the company. A key distinction of a C Corp. is that the income is generally taxed. Large companies generally (Nike, Dell, Apple, etc.) are C Corporations.

StartUp Step 8: Answer the following questions to help select a legal structure:

1> Will you be the only owner of the business or will there be shared ownership?

KEEP IT GOING

LEARN MORE ABOUT ESTABLISHING LEGAL STRUCTURES AND OTHER OPERATIONAL DETAILS **AT WWW.STARTINGUPNOW.COM.**

2> Do you plan to start the business with your own money? Will you secure a loan? Should you consider selling a portion of the business in exchange for investment capital?

3> Do you plan to grow, expand, or sell the business in the first 1–3 years?

4> Should you be concerned with protecting your personal assets (home, savings, automobiles, etc.) in the event that you are sued?

5> Who will be your legal advisor?

Maxim: "You need a plan to build a house. To build a life, it is more important to have a plan or goal."
—Zig Ziglar

MYLEG

STARTING UP KEY 9

MANAGEMENT TEAM

Description: *Introduce the management team by providing the following information: Name(s) and Title(s), Direct Responsibilities, Previous Experience, and Whom They Report To.*

Model

Custom Bikes MGMT Team

Julian Millard, Owner—Julian is responsible for all aspects of Custom Bikes, design, manufacturing, and client relations. Julian has been in the biking industry for over 20 years and has won numerous industry awards. Julian reports to Custom Bikes' investors.

Omar Reyes, Designer—Omar creates custom bike designs for customers desiring unique bicycles. Omar's designs have won awards for the past 10 years. Omar reports to the Owner.

Megan Smith, Dir. of Advertising—Megan is responsible for the design of all print and web-based advertising tools. Megan has worked at Custom Bikes for the last three years and reports to the Director of Sales.

Chelesta Falcone, Sales—Chelesta is responsible for managing independent sales reps throughout the United States and Canada. Chelesta has worked at Custom Bikes for the past six months and reports to the Owner.

StartUp Key 9: Your company's management structure and style will define its culture. Your leadership team should create and foster a productive environment for growth and communication. Establishing accountability early is critical for productive business operations.

Use the following leadership structure (1–5) to help establish the person, his or her position, and whom he or she reports to. Substitute the appropriate position titles as you see fit.

1> Owner/CEO

2> Finance/Accounting

KEEP IT GOING — LEARN STRATEGIES TO DEVELOP YOUR LEADERSHIP SKILLS AT WWW.STARTINGUPNOW.COM.

3> Sales/Marketing

4> Operations

5> Customer Relations

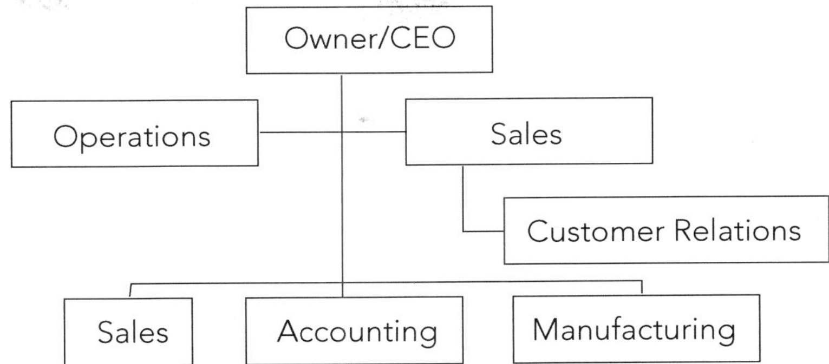

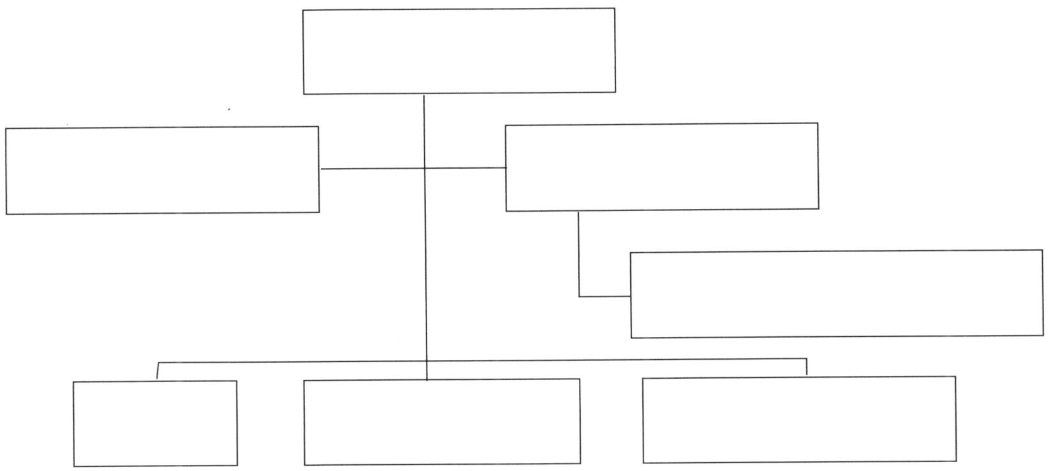

Maxim: "Leadership is the essence of any organized structure. Leaders must lead, follow, or get out of the way."
—Thomas Paine

YEARONE GOALS & ACTIVITIES

Description: *Your business goals should be attainable yet compel you to work hard to realize them. Goals provide specific focus that can be measured over a period of time. Achieving goals gives a sense of accomplishment and positive energy.*

Models

The Lincoln Café Goals

Short-Term Goals (1–6 months):

> Secure monthly lease in strategic location to operate.
> Hire one hosts, five waiters/waitresses, three cooks;
> Identify 100 weekly repeat customers;
> Break Even by 2nd Quarter

Long Term Goals (six months–one year):

> Grow my weekly repeat customer base to 200 customers;
> Sign a three-year lease with an option to purchase location;
> Hire restaurant manager with at least five years of experience
> Generate $25,000 in net profits

StartUp Step 10: Use the following questions to guide the process for determining your goals for each of the time periods listed below.

1> Articulate your goals.

2> Identify the benchmarks to achieving your goals. Describe Your Goal and be as specific as possible.

3> Establish a deadline for the goal to be completed.

4> Explain why achieving the goals will be important to the business.

5> Recognize obstacles that may prevent you from achieving each goal.

6> Upon successfully completing the goal, identify what you learned.

KEEP IT GOING — READ ABOUT HOW OTHER COMPANIES DETERMINE THEIR GOALS AT WWW.STARTINGUPNOW.COM.

Maxim: "Many are the plans in a man's heart, but it is the LORD's purpose that prevails."
—Proverbs 19:21, New International Version

MYYOGA

INDUSTRYANALYSIS

Description: Investors need to know what's happening in your industry. Provide information on industry potential, competition, growth, and innovations.

Mode

Red Line Race Works (Atlanta): Industry Trends for Slot Car Racing

Model slot car racing is a reemerging industry for model car racing hobbyist. It was first popularized in the '60s and gained visibility as commercial tracks sprung up in the U.S. and throughout Europe. The 1/32 scale is the most popular scale at this present time. There are approximately nine commercial tracks in the Atlanta area that range in size from 30–250 square feet. Scalextric distributed by Hornby controls about 70% of the U.S. market while other industry leaders, such as Carrera, Slot-It, and Fly, make up the balance. There is little government regulation as this is a very safe and non-technical industry. As we prepare to open three additional locations in the Charlotte, Orlando, and Birmingham areas, we will also introduce web-based racing simulations.

StartUp Step 11: Use the following questions to serve as a guide to identify the trends in your industry.

1> How many businesses are in your industry?

2> How much revenue does your industry generate annually?

3> Who are the industry leaders?

4> What is your position in the industry?

5> What are the existing government regulations for your industry?

6> Are there any threats to the industry?

7> Are there any foreseeable changes in your industry's immediate future?

KEEP IT GOING

COLLECT INDUSTRY-SPECIFIC INTELLIGENCE AND SHARE YOUR EXPERIENCE AT WWW.STARTINGUPNOW.COM.

Maxim: Tell your story. What do you know about this industry that will give you a competitive edge? By telling your story and your niche, you can also provide an effective, passionate analysis of your industry that's both compelling and informative.

MYIA

MARKETING

Description: *Marketing is the activities and methods the business owner uses to sell their products or services to their customers. In order to have a solid business plan, the business owner must conduct market research.*

Model

West Side Geeks, Inc.

West Side Geeks, Inc., is conducting market research to determine if their idea of refurbishing and reselling pre-owned computers will lead to a profitable business. In order to determine their likelihood of success, they must research their potential market. What they learn from their market research will help create effective marketing strategies, techniques, and tools needed to communicate the value of their product or service to potential customers.

The Six P's of Marketing People, Product, Price, Place, Promotion, and Presentation will help West Side Geeks, Inc., learn more about their market. Here's a brief description of the Six P's.

1> People—Undervaluing people in your business activities will likely lead to the failure of the business. What do they need your product or service to do? How are they valued in the process?

2> Product—Clearly identify what you are selling. Is it a product/service? How will the customer benefit from the product/service?

3> Price—How much are customers willing to pay? How much are they currently paying for the same or a similar product?

4> Place—Where are customers currently purchasing the same or similar service?

5> Promotion—How is the product/service currently being promoted?

6> Presentation—How and where is the product/service being presented?

KEEP IT GOING | JOIN THE COMMUNITY OF NEW ENTREPRENEURS AT WWW.STARTINGUPNOW.COM.

By researching the Six P's of Marketing, West Side Geeks, Inc., learned the following about their potential market:

People	> Parents value their children's education. > They want to purchase an affordable computer for their children to do their homework and use online educational tools. > Most parents are lower to middle income and work full-time.
Product	> Customers want a reliable desktop computer that includes (keyboard, mouse, display, CPU). > A major brand is helpful but not necessary. > Some level of product support and warranty is desired—especially for refurbished computers. > Installation and networking the computer would be helpful.
Price	> Customers are willing to pay $350–$600 for a desktop computer. > Some customers purchase on credit or layaway.
Place	> Currently most customers purchase only from big box retailers.
Promotion	> Big box retailers run weekly ads in local newspapers and advertise using social media. > Flyers, business cards, and other advertising tools.
Presentation	> Packaging used is not environmentally responsible. > Some computer components are manufactured with products that are harmful to the environment.

Let's perform market research for your own business. Using the chart on the following page as a guide, research 2–3 companies that offer the same/similar products and services just as West Side Geeks, Inc., did.

STARTING UP KEY 12

MARKETING

	COMPANY 1	COMPANY 2	COMPANY 3
People:			
Product:			
Price:			
Place:			
Promotion:			
Presentation:			

KEEP IT GOING

JOIN THE COMMUNITY OF NEW ENTREPRENEURS AT WWW.STARTINGUPNOW.COM.

StartUp Step 12: Now that you've conducted research on similar businesses selling the same product or service, let's focus on your own business. Using the Six P's as a guide to market your own business, identify the People, Product, Price, Place, Promotion, and Presentation for your own business.

People:	
Product:	
Price:	
Place:	
Promotion:	
Presentation:	

Maxim: "Strategy without tactics is the slowest route to victory. Tactics without strategy is the noise before defeat."

—*Sun Tzu*

TARGET CUSTOMER PROFILE

Description: *An expert understanding of your customers and prospects is critical to developing your sales strategy and future development of new products and services.*

Models

Meraz Miniature Golf (MMG) Customer Profile

MMG is a seasonal, family-owned-and-operated miniature golf complex located in a major metropolitan city with approximately 150,000 working families within a five-mile radius. Each year MMG attracts customers that are typically multi-ethnic families with an annual income of $40,000–$75,000 and have children between the ages of 5–12 years old. The average family of four will spend $25.00 on golfing and an additional $20.00 on food and beverages for 36 holes of golfing. MMG is often viewed as an affordable alternative that is in closer proximity than the major amusement park, which is about 40 miles away. MMG customers value a clean, safe, family-friendly environment that's affordable for working families. MMG also provides birthday parties, private and corporate events, and weekly contests, along with family membership passes throughout the summer.

StartUp Step 13: Let the following questions serve as a guide to create a profile of your customers.

1> What are the demographics of your target market: income level, age range, education level, disposable income, gender, race/ethnicity, location, etc.?

2> What are the psychographics of the target market: values, social class, lifestyle, and personality characteristics?

3> How large is your target market? Is this a niche/specialty market?

4> On what do your potential customers spend money?

5> From where do they currently purchase the product or service that you provide?

KEEP IT GOING FOR ADDITIONAL RESOURCES AND IDEAS ON CREATING YOUR TARGET CUSTOMER PROFILE, LOG ON TO **WWW.STARTINGUPNOW.COM.**

Maxim: "With businesses, you go to the same places because you like the service, you like the people, and they take care of you. They greet you with a smile. That's how people want to be treated, with respect. That's what I tell my employees...customer service is very important."
—Erving "Magic" Johnson

MYTCP

STARTING UP KEY 14

FEATURES & BENEFITS

Description: *Highlighting the features and benefits of your product or service is a necessity. It's important to identify multiple FEATURES and show how the features will directly BENEFIT the customer.*

Model

Disposable Pen:

FEATURES	····>	**BENEFITS**
Inexpensive	····>	Affordable to most consumers
Clip	····>	Attaches to pocket or folder
Disposable	····>	Inexpensive to own
Multiple colors of ink	····>	Various colors for different tasks
Small/Compact	····>	Easy to carry
Comes with a cap	····>	Reduces ink spillage
Name Brand	····>	Trustworthy brand/Reliability
Sold at Retail Stores	····>	Available

StartUp Key 14: Identify the features and benefits of your product or service in the columns below:

FEATURES	····>	**BENEFITS**
	····>	
	····>	
	····>	
	····>	
	····>	
	····>	
	····>	
	····>	

KEEP IT GOING

GAIN PRODUCT PROMOTION TECHNIQUES AND BEST PRACTICES AT WWW.STARTINGUPNOW.COM.

Maxim: "Always be truth-telling. A half-truth is a whole lie."
—Yiddish Proverb

MYFAB

SALESSTRATEGY

ABBREVIATION

SELL

Description: *Developing your sales strategy is an essential task. As an entrepreneur, this is your opportunity to define your company's approach to prospect identification, account generation, and achieving sales targets.*

Model

CleanStic Toothpicks, Inc.

Tagline: Only clean the teeth you want to keep!
Sales Pitch: CleanStic Toothpicks provide oral hygiene cleanliness, breath enhancers, along with being environmentally safe. At the conclusion of each meal, simply remove the CleanStic from the biodegradable wrapping and swiftly clean the surfaces and crevices between your teeth. By removing excess particles of food, immediately patrons reduce the possible plaque buildup along with minimizing bad breath from food particles left in the mouth. Which flavor of CleanStic would you like to try?

StartUp Step 15:

> **S**how the feature and demonstrate how the feature works.

> **E**xplain how the customer will benefit from the advantage gained from the feature.

> **L**ead into the features and benefits. Demonstrate how it will benefit their direct need.

> **L**et the customer talk among themselves about how the product will benefit them; if done correctly they will talk themselves into a sell.

Maxim: "For every sale you miss because you're too enthusiastic, you'll miss a hundred because you are not enthusiastic enough. Every sale has five basic obstacles: no need, no money, no hurry, no desire, no trust."
—*Zig Ziglar*

KEEP IT GOING — LEARN ADDITIONAL SALES TIPS AND STRATEGIES ONLINE AT WWW.STARTINGUPNOW.COM.

MYCOMPETITION

Description: *Knowing your competition provides valuable information. You must know who they are and where they are located. Identifying each competitor's strengths and weaknesses allows you to demonstrate why customers will select your product over your competitors. Knowing your competition will allow for better knowledge of your industry and target customer.*

Model

Below is a chart highlighting the competitive differences between three stores that retail similar products. There are pros and cons to purchasing the product from one or the other.

Product: Toaster	Local Store	National Chain	Specialty Store
Quality	Average	Good	Excellent
Reputation	Good	Average	Excellent
Customer Service	Good	Below Average	Excellent
Selection	1–3	1–10	1–5
Price Point	$15.00–$30.00	$10.00–$40.00	$40.00–200.00
Product Knowledge	Average	Below Average	Excellent

StartUp Key 16: In order to best compete with your competition, use the following steps to analyze your competition and let's prepare your strategy to compete:

1> Who currently sells the same or similar product or service as you?

2> What is the size of the target market?

3> What factors are most important to the customers when making a decision (price, quality, selection, warranty, etc.)?

Maxim: "Make your product easier to buy than your competition, or you will find your customers buying from them, not you."
—*Mark Cuban*

KEEP IT GOING — NEED ADDITIONAL STRATEGIES TO DEAL WITH YOUR COMPETITION? VISIT **WWW.STARTINGUPNOW.COM** TO LEARN MORE.

MYCOMP

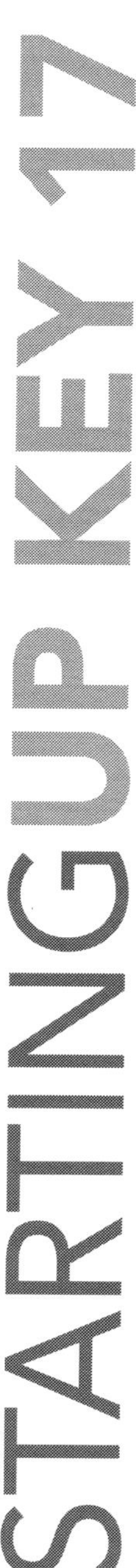

S.W.O.T.S.

Description: *Identifying and acting on your advantages is a useful strategy not only in starting your business but also in order to remain competitive in the marketplace. We often spend far too much time focusing on our weaknesses versus recognizing and building on our strengths.*

Models

Prime Ribs management is accessing their marketplace position through a S.W.O.T.S. analysis. Below is their internal S.W.O.T.S. review:

S.W.O.T.S.	Prime Ribs S.W.O.T.S. Analysis
Strengths: Identify all of your strengths that positively impact your business.	> Profitable & Well-Organized > Family-Friendly Reputation > National Awards > Secret Sauce/Recipe
Weaknesses: Identify your areas of weakness that need to be improved.	> Limited Access to Capital > Small Location > Employee Turnover
Opportunities: Which opportunities exist that can improve your business.	> Small Business Loan > Expansion to 2nd Location > Retail Sauce in Grocery Stores
Threats: Identify internal/external threats that could negatively impact your business.	> Lack of Access to Capital > New construction project impacting traffic flow
Strategies: List out your strategies to overcome your weaknesses and minimize your threats.	> Sell 30% of business to secure investment capital > Increase hourly wage to reduce turnover

KEEP IT GOING — LEARN MORE ABOUT "STRENGTH COACHING AND TECHNIQUES" AT **WWW.STARTINGUPNOW.COM.**

StartUp Step 17: Let's begin to identify your strengths by completing a SWOTS analysis on your new start-up.

S.W.O.T.S.	My Business
Strengths: Identify all of your strengths that positively impact your business.	> > > >
Weaknesses: Identify your areas of weakness that need to be improved.	> > >
Opportunities: Which opportunities exist that can improve your business?	> > >
Threats: Identify internal/external threats that could negatively impact your business.	> >
Strategies: List out your strategies to overcome your weaknesses and minimize your threats.	> >

Maxim: "It doesn't matter who you are or where you come from. The ability to triumph begins with you. Always."
—Oprah Winfrey

MY S.W.O.T.S.

STARTING UP KEY 18

MYADVERTISING

Description: *Advertising is truthfully communicating a message to persuade customers to purchase your product or service.*

Model
Product: TAZE!
Slogan: Power Drinks for Triathletes
Tagline: Get Your TAZE ON!

Script: Train harder, run faster, swim longer, bike harder—outlast your competition with TAZE Power Drinks.

StartUp Step 18: Advertising often takes the form of television and radio commercials, Facebook and YouTube banner ads, slogans, brochures, and business cards. Use the following questions to help you create a memorable, truthful ad about your product or service.

Create a 30-Second Ad:

1> Identify your product/service that you are selling.

2> Create a slogan that ties in with your product/service.

3> Create a memorable tag line that they won't forget.

4> Write out the script. Keep it short; you only have 30 seconds.

5> Perform the ad. If needed, use friends and props.

6> Record the ad with a video or webcam.

7> Edit the ad with simple software and post it on YouTube.

Hint: Use your FAB & SELL sections to complete your commercial.

Maxim: "Do not deceive one another."
—Leviticus 19:11, New International Version

KEEP IT GOING | CHECK OUT OTHER ADVERTISING TOOLS AND TECHNIQUES AT WWW.STARTINGUPNOW.COM.

Description: *Start-up cost is the amount of money needed to purchase the items necessary to start your business.*

Models

Michelle of Old Time Lemonade is setting up "just outside the fence" of a professional football team's training camp facilities in the Midwest. Many fans visit the facility to watch the team practice. Michelle wants to make $500.00 in one day to purchase a new computer for the upcoming school year. Below, she's listed the items needed to start the lemonade stand. She's selling her lemonade for $3.00 per cup—no free refills.

Old Time Lemonade Start-up Costs:

Item	Unit Cost	Quantity	Total
Lemons	.20 each	20	$4.00
Bottled Water	$2.00	20	$40.00
Pitcher	$3.00	2	$6.00
Mixing Spoon	$1.00	2	$2.00
Signage for Posters	$1.00	5	$5.00
Lemonade Mix	$5.00	5	$25.00
Cups (12 oz.)	$3.00	8 (24 in pkg.)	$24.00
Ice (20 lb. bag)	$3.00	2	$6.00
Table & 2 Chairs	$20.00	1	20.00
Hourly Pay Rate	$5.00	8	$40.00
Total			$172.00

StartUp Step 19: The questions and chart to the right will guide you through the beginning stages of determining your Start-up Costs.

1> Create a list of all the items you need to get your business started for one month. This will be the beginning of your inventory list.

KEEP IT GOING

JOIN THE COMMUNITY OF NEW ENTREPRENEURS AT WWW.STARTINGUPNOW.COM.

2> Next, write down the quantity of the items needed for each of the items.

3> List out the approximate costs next to each of the items.

4> Typically, when you are a *licensed* business owner reselling a product or service, you can receive a *wholesale* discount that ranges from 30–60% off retail price. These discounts typically apply when you purchase in *bulk* quantities. List out the *vendor's* name and the discount percentage they are offering you.

Item	Unit Cost	Quantity	Vendor	Discount %	Sub-Total

MYSUC

OPERATIONAL EXPENSES

Description: *Operational expenses are the budgeted costs that are incurred in order for the business to remain functional. These expenses typically occur each month regardless of how many products or services the business sells. OPEX is often referred to as* Fixed Costs *because they occur each month. For example, whether a clothing store sells 50 or 500 shirts, the store must pay rent each month. Knowing and planning for your monthly operational expenses is vital for operations. OPEX are also called* Overhead.

Model

High End Fashions, LLC., is a used clothing store that sells only the latest women's fashions. It is extremely important for High End to know its OPEX to effectively budget and plan for future months. See the example below.

USAIIRM	Description	High End USAIIRM
for June		
U-tilities	Electric, Gas, Phone, Cell, Internet	$300.00
S-alaries	Employee Payroll & Payroll Taxes	$2,000.00
A-dvertising	Ads, Coupons, Web Banner Ads, etc.	$500.00
I-nsurance	General Insurance for the business	$50.00
I-nterest	Business Loan Payments	$100.00
R-ent	Rent or Mortgage Payment	$500.00
M-iscellaneous	Uncategorized Expenses	$50.00
Total		$3,500.00

The owners of High End Fashions know that each month their operational expenses will be at least $3500. Knowing their operational expenses helps to create a strategy in order for the business to be profitable.

StartUp Step 20: Use USAIIRM to budget your monthly operational expenses with the chart on the right. Use the following questions to get started:

1> What will I spend on utilities each month?

KEEP IT GOING — JOIN THE COMMUNITY OF NEW ENTREPRENEURS AT WWW.STARTINGUPNOW.COM.

2> How much will I budget for salaries each month?

3> Do I plan to advertise this month? If so, how much will I budget?

4> How much will the business spend per month on insurance expenses?

5> If the business has a loan, how much needs to be paid back per month?

6> How much is your rent each month?

7> Do you want to budget a certain amount for uncategorized expenses? If so, how much?

Maxim: "Take care of the pennies and the dollars will take care of themselves."
—William Lowndes, U.S. Congressman

U-tilities	Budgeted Amount
S-alaries	
A-dvertising	
I-nsurance	
I-nterest	
R-ent	
M-iscellaneous	
Total	

MYOPEX

COST OF GOODS

Description: *Knowing your Cost of Goods (COG) is essential for setting the prices of your products or services. COG is the cost the business pays to make the products/services available. COG typically includes the cost of things such as material and labor.*

Model

Jamal's Donuts

Jamal sells donuts at school. Jamal sells his donuts for $1.00 each (a). Jamal purchases donuts wholesale on average for about $0.30 per donut (b). Therefore Jamal's COGS is $0.30 per unit, and he makes $0.70 in *gross profit* (c).

Retail Price (a) - COGS (b) = Gross Profit (c)

Jamal's COGS		
Donut Retail Price	$1.00	*a*
Cost of Goods Sold	$0.30	*b*
Gross Profit per donut	$0.70	*c*

DSX Wooden Deck Washing Service

David and Shawn own and operate a deck washing service. DSX sells a service (deck washing) but must include the cost of supplies (products) needed to clean the decks. They charge $100.00 per deck (a). The hourly rate they pay themselves is $10.00 per hour (b), and it takes two hours to perform the service (c) for a total labor cost of $20.00 per person (d). The men must also factor in the cost of supplies (e) needed to perform the job, and they *mark up* their supply cost by 15% (f). They combine their supply cost and markup percentage (g) to get their total supply cost of $57.50. By subtracting their COS (h) from their retail price (a), their gross profit is $22.50 (i).

KEEP IT GOING

TO LEARN MORE ABOUT OPERATIONAL EXPENSES AT WWW.STARTINGUPNOW.COM.

DSX Cost of Services (COS)		
Deck Washing Retail Price	$100.00	*a*
Labor Cost Per Hour	$10.00	*b*
How Many Hours To Perform Service	2	*c*
Total Labor Cost	$20.00	*d*
Cost of Supplies	$10.00	*e*
Supplies Markup 15%	$5.00	*f*
Supplies + Markup	$15.50	*g*
Cost of Services Sold	$35.50	*h*
Gross Profit	$65.50	*i*

They combine their supply cost and markup percentage (e+f) to get their total supply and labor cost of $35.00 (h). Now, by subtracting their Total Supply & Labor Cost (a-i) they get their gross profit of $65.00 (i).

MYCOG

INCOMESTATEMENT

Description: *The Income Statement (INST) reports on the amount of revenue a company has earned over a specific period of time. The INST allows the business owner to review detailed information on where the business is making or losing money. The INST is also referred to as the Profit & Loss Statement (P&L).*

Model

Green Acres Landscaping—Monthly Income Statement

Green Acres provides seasonal landscaping services in the southeastern region of the United States. Green Acres' target customer is middle to upper income families. Let's break down Green Acres income statement for the month of June.

Sales: Green Acres made $5,000 in sales.

COS/COGS: Expenses for products/services needed to perform the service is $1,000.00.

Gross Profit: Sales-Cost of Goods Sold. After subtracting COS/COGS, Green Acres gross profit is $4,000 before subtracting Operating Expenses (OPEX).

OPEX: Fixed Costs + Variable Costs are the expenses the business must pay each month to operate. Total Fixed and Variable Costs to get the Total Operational Costs for the month.

Variable Cost–> Expenses that vary with the amount of product or services sold. A good rule of thumb is to budget 10% for variable expenses. Green Acres VC is $500.00.

Fixed Cost–> USAIIRM expenses that must be paid each month. Green Acres FC is $780.00.

KEEP IT GOING

LEARN MORE ABOUT INCOME STATEMENTS AT WWW.STARTINGUPNOW.COM.

Profit Less OPEX: Subtracting the OPEX expenses from the Gross Profit will let you know how much revenue the business has generated after OPEX has been paid. In Green Acres' case, OPEX totals $1,280.00.

Charitable Contribution: A portion of the profits a business donates to a charity. This helps the business support not-for-profit organizations in the community and also reduces federal taxes paid. Green Acres also builds *goodwill,* which helps grow its *Brand.* Green Acres donates 10% of its profits or $272.00 in June, to a charity each month.

Profits Before Taxes: Upon subtracting the Charitable Contribution Green Acres now knows its taxable income that must be paid to the government. Green Acres' taxable income is $2,448.00.

Taxes: Government expenses the business must pay to support the country. Taxes pay for schools, roads, clean water, military, police, and other systems necessary for a country to operate. Green Acres must pay $625.00 in taxes.

Net Profit: The amount the business makes after all operational expenses, charitable contributions, and taxes have been subtracted. This is often referred to as the *Bottom Line* since it's the last line on the INC. This is the amount of money the business owner pays himself/herself, distributes to the ownership, and/or *Reinvests* back into the business. Green Acres' net profit is $1,836.00.

INCOMESTATEMENT

ABBREVIATION
INST

Total Revenue			
Sales			$5,000.00
Cost of Goods Sold			$1,000.00
Gross Profit			$4,000.00
Operating Expenses			
Variable Cost (10% of Sales)			$5000.00
Fixed Costs			$780.00
	Utilities	$50.00	
	Salaries	$500.00	
	Advertising	$0.00	
	Insurance	$50.00	
	Interest	$50.00	
	Rent	$100.00	
	Miscellaneous	$30.00	
Total Operating Expenses			**$1,280.00**
Profit Less Operating Expenses			$2,720.00
Charitable Contribution (10%)			$272.00
Profit Before Income Taxes			$2448.00
Income Taxes (25%)			$612.00
Net Profit			**$1,836.00**

StartUp Step 22: Use the following questions to help guide you through developing an income statement for your business for one month. Use the template on page 58 to record your answers.

1> What are your Sales for this month?

2> What are your COGS/COS for this month?

3> Now, subtract your COGS/COS from Sales. This is your Gross Profit.

KEEP IT GOING

LEARN MORE ABOUT FINANCIAL STATEMENTS AND ONLINE TOOLS **AT WWW.STARTINGUPNOW.COM.**

4> OPEX
   a. Variable Cost is 10% of your Sales. Determine 10% of your sales and use that amount to budget for your Variable Cost.
   b. Fixed Cost are your OPEX. Use USAIIRM to determine your OPEX.
   c. Add both your Variable Cost + Fixed Cost to get your Total OPEX.

5> Next, you need to subtract Total OPEX from Gross Profit. Put the sum of that amount as your Profit Less Operating Expenses.

6> Now, it's time to determine the amount of your Charitable Contribution, which also reduces your taxable income. We'll use 10% to get started. Determine 10% of your Profit Less Operating Expenses. That's the amount you will donate.

7> Next, subtract the amount of your Charitable Contribution and enter that amount in the Profit Before Income Taxes. That amount is now what your Income Taxes will be based on.

8> Now, it's time to determine the amount of taxes the business must pay. The amount of your taxes is based on the percentage of the businesses income. The higher your income, the more you pay in taxes. The lower your income, the less you pay in taxes. For this purpose, let's plan on 25% of your income being taxed. Go ahead and determine 25% of Profit Before Taxes and write that amount in Income Taxes.

9> Finally, to determine your Net Profit, subtract the amount of your Income Taxes from Profit before Income Taxes and that's your Net Profit.

In a traditional Income Statement charitable contributions are NOT included. However, to encourage donating financial resources to charitable organizations, this has intentionally been included. Please remove this line if you opt to follow a more traditional approach.

Maxim: "I don't like money actually, but it quiets my nerves."
—***Joe Louis, World Champion Boxer***

STARTING UP KEY 22

INCOME STATEMENT

ABBREVIATION
INST

Total Revenue			
Sales			
Cost of Goods Sold			
Gross Profit			
Operating Expenses			
Variable Cost (10% of Sales)			
Fixed Costs			
	Utilities		
	Salaries		
	Advertising		
	Insurance		
	Interest		
	Rent		
	Miscellaneous		
Total Operating Expenses			
Profit Less Operating Expenses			
Charitable Contribution (10%)			
Profit Before Income Taxes			
Income Taxes (25%)			
Net Profit			

KEEP IT GOING

JOIN THE COMMUNITY OF NEW ENTREPRENEURS AT WWW.STARTINGUPNOW.COM.

MYINST

BALANCESHEET

STARTINGUP KEY 23

Description: *The Balance Sheet (BAL) provides the financial position of the business on any given date. It's essentially a "financial checkup" and gives the business owner instant information as to the overall "health" of the business.*

Model

Let's take a look at Green Acres Landscaping's BAL to get an idea of the company's overall health.

Green Acres Balance Sheet—December 31, 2009

	31-Dec	30-Jun
Assets		
Current Assets		
Checking/Savings	$7,962.28	$2,300.00
Accounts Receivable	$200.00	$500.00
Total Inventory Assets	$1,000.00	$2,000.00
Total Current Assets	*$9,162.28*	*$4,800.00*
Fixed Assets		
Equipment	$450.00	$500.00
Computers	$900.00	$1,000.00
Printers	$180.00	$200.00
Telephones	$90.00	$100.00
Total Fixed Assets	$1350.00	$1500.00
Total Current & Fixed Assets	*$20,596.53*	*$6,300.00*
Liabilities & Equity		
Current Liabilities		
Accounts Payable	$500.00	$1,000.00
Other Current Liabilities	$500.00	$2,500.00
Total Current Liabilities	*$500.00*	*$2,500.00*
Opening Balance Equity	$20,000.00	$3,800.00
Retained Earnings	$96.53	$0.00
Owner's Equity (Company's Net Worth)	*$20,096.53*	
Total Liabilities & Equity	$20,596.53	$6,300.00

KEEP IT GOING

JOIN THE COMMUNITY OF NEW ENTREPRENEURS AT WWW.STARTINGUPNOW.COM.

Assets: Assets represent ownership of items that may be converted or sold to create cash value.

Current Assets are assets that are usually sold or used up as part of the business operation.

Green Acres' Current Assets as of December 31, 2009

Checking/Savings Account: Cash is considered an asset because of its value. Green Acres Landscaping had $7,962 in its checking/savings account on Dec. 31.

Accounts Receivable (AR): Typically cash that's owed to your company for selling your products/services that's been *Invoiced* to your customer. Most AR has a Net 30 term, meaning payment is due in 30 days. Green Acres has $200.00 in its AR.

Total Inventory Assets: The cash value of your inventory. Green Acres has $1,000 in inventory.

Total Current Assets: Totaling the Checking/Savings Account, AP, and Inventory gives the cash value of your Total Current Assets. Green Acres' Total Current Assets are $9,162.

Fixed Assets are properties that the business owns that can be converted into cash. They are called fixed because they are "nailed" down to the floor.

Green Acres' Fixed Assets as of December 31, 2009

Fixed Assets: Equipment, Computers, Telephone, Printers, Trucks. Green Acres' fixed assets have a cash value of $6,730.

Total Current Assets

Fixed Assets: Provides you with the total cash value of the business. Green Acres has a worth of $15, 532.

Liabilities & Equity: A liability is a debt that the business owes. Equity is the value of ownership in the company.

Current Liabilities: Debts the business owes that are to be paid within the year.

Green Acres Liabilities as of December 31, 2009

Accounts Payable (AP): Products purchased or services used by Green Acres for which they owe. Green Acres' current AP is $500.00.

Other Current Liabilities: Consists of expenses that will take longer than a year to be paid, such as a lease or mortgage. Green Acres' Other Current Liability is a $1,500 equipment lease.

Current Equity: The total value of the owner's interest in the company.

Retained Earnings: The amount of cash that's kept in the business and not distributed to owners or shareholders in the company. Green Acres retained earnings is $96.00.

Company Net Worth: The Opening Balance Equity plus the Retained Earnings equals the business's net worth. Green Acres has a net worth of $20,096.

StartUp Step 23: Use the following questions to help guide you in determining your business assets. Record your answers using the chart on page 64.

1> How much will you deposit into your business banking account? Enter that amount under the Beginning Period—Checking/Savings.

2> If you have any current payments that are owed to you, enter that under Beginning Period—Accounts Receivable (AR).

3> If you know the total of your Inventory Assets, enter that under Beginning Period—Total Inventory Assets.

4> Now total your assets to get your Total Current Assets and enter that amount under Beginning Period—Total Current Assets.

5> Follow the same procedure for the following for the Fixed Assets and then total the amount and enter it under Beginning Period—Total Current & Fixed Assets.

KEEP IT GOING

JOIN THE COMMUNITY OF NEW ENTREPRENEURS AT WWW.STARTINGUPNOW.COM.

Now, let's determine your business' Liabilities & Equity.

1> Under the Beginning Period column, list any outstanding bills. Total these and enter the amount under Accounts Payable (AP).

2> Under the Beginning Period –Other Current Liabilities, total up any long-term, outstanding debts (longer than 12 months) and enter them here.

3> Now total your AP and Other Current Liabilities and enter the total amount under Beginning Period—Total Current Liabilities

Next, let's determine your ownership stake in the business.

1> Under the Beginning Period column, enter the Opening Balance Equity.

2> Under the Beginning Period column, enter the Retained Earnings. There may not be any earnings since you are just starting.

3> Total Opening Balance Equity + Retained Earnings and you have your Company's Net Worth.

As your business grows, sales will be made and expenses incurred. The BAL will reflect the overall health of your business. Many businesses review their Balance Sheet at the end of each *Fiscal Quarter*. The Balance Sheet provides critical information when analyzing your business growth and progress. It also identifies areas for improvement.

Maxim: "A healthy balance sheet can lead to a restful and relaxing sleep for the business owner."
—Author Unknown

STARTING UP KEY 23

BALANCE SHEET

	End Period	Beg Period
Assets		
Current Assets		
Checking/Savings		
Accounts Receivable		
Total Inventory Assets		
Total Current Assets		
Fixed Assets		
Equipment		
Computers		
Printers		
Telephones		
Total Fixed Assets		
Total Current & Fixed Assets		
Liabilities & Equity		
Current Liabilities		
Accounts Payable		
Other Current Liabilities		
Total Current Liabilities		
Opening Balance Equity		
Retained Earnings		
Owner's Equity (Company's Net Worth)		
Total Liabilities & Equity		

KEEP IT GOING

CHECK OUT THE BALANCE SHEET TEMPLATES AND OTHER RESOURCES AT **WWW.STARTINGUPNOW.COM.**

MYBAL

STARTING UP KEY 24

CASHFLOW

Description: *The movement of cash in and out of the business over a specific period of time. Cash flow helps the business owner track the overall health of the business.*

Model

Sergio Gonzalez has owned and operated, ALG Designs, Inc., (ALGD), an Advertising Agency, in Chicago for the past six years. He's grown the company from operating in his basement with 1 client to 17 clients and five employees. He's considering opening an office in New York and needs to secure capital for expansion. Potential banks and investors want to review his financials, particularly his cash flow, statement to get an idea of ALGD's financial position. Let's review the Cash Flow statement in detail.

1> For Year Ending December 31, 2009—This is the period of time that is covered in the cash flow statement. It provides the exact information of the business's activities during that period.

2> Cash at Beginning of Period—This is the total amount of cash the business had on January 1, 2009.

3> Operating Activities—ALGD's business activities from January–December 31, 2009.

a. Net Income—the total amount of income from sales for the specific period. ALGD generated $235,000 in net income.

b. Cash Paid for—Items listed here are the specific operating expenses broken down by their category.

i. Inventory Purchases—Total expenses for inventory purchased for that specific period. ALG Designs spent $50,000 in inventory.

ii. Operational Expenses (OPEX)—-ALG Designs expenses for the business's -operations for that specific period. ALG Designs spent $175,000 in operational expenses.

KEEP IT GOING | VIEW CASH FLOW STATEMENTS BY INDUSTRY AT WWW.STARTINGUPNOW.COM.

iii. Salaries—the total amount ALG Designs paid to employees for that specific period.

c. Net Cash Provided by Operating Expenses—to determine this amount do the following: Net Income – Operational Expenses = Net Cash provided by Operating Expenses.

4> **Investing Activities**—the amount of money the business has spent or received from all investment activities.

a. Cash Receipts from—the amount of income received from the sale of the business's assets.

i. Sale of Equipment or Property—the amount received from the sale of equipment or property. ALGD sold $15,000 worth of equipment in 2009.

ii. Sale of Investment Securities—These are typically purchased for investment purposes. Since ALGD needs capital to expand the business, they sold $20,000 worth of stocks and bonds held in other companies.

b. Cash Paid for—the itemized amount the business paid for physical assets for the business's operations.

i. Purchase of Equipment—ALGD spent $10,000 on equipment purchases.

ii. Loans to Others—ALGD loaned $1,500 to a local small business.

iii. Purchase of Investment Securities—ALGD did not purchase investment securities during this period since they needed cash to expand the business.

c. Net Cash Provided by Investment Activities—to determine this amount, do the following: Cash Receipts – Cash Paid = Net Cash Provided by Investment Activities.

5> **Financing Activities**—where the business reports the amount of money it spent or received from stocks, bonds, or loans used to finance its activities.

a. Cash Receipts from Issuance of Stock—this is the amount of cash a business receives if it sold a portion of the business to raise cash. In the case of ALG Designs, Sergio Gonzalez, used his own money to finance ALG Designs and still owns 100% of the company. *As long as the owner owns 51% of the company, they control the company.*

i. ALGD received no cash from issuing any stocks.

b. Cash Receipts from Loans—is the amount of cash a business receives for any repayments.

i. ALGD received a $1,000 loan payment in 2009.

c. Cash Paid for Purchase of Stock—this is the amount of cash a business pays for any stocks or bonds it purchases.
    i. ALGD did not purchase any stock in 2009.
d. Cash Paid for Loan Repayments—the amount of cash a business pays for any loans.
    i. ALGD repaid $10,000 in a loan payment. This also helped reduce their total debt, which is looked upon favorably when seeking investment capital.
e. Dividends to Investors—a dividend is the distribution of profits to owners (shareholders) of the business.
    i. Since ALGD is 100% owned by Sergio Gonzalez, he is entitled to 100% of the profits of ALGD. If Mr. Gonzalez sells a portion of the company—let's say 5%—he would then have to pay the other owners 5% of the profits.
f. Net Cash Provided by Financing Activities—to determine the amount do the following: Cash Receipts – Cash Paid for (Expenses) = Net Cash provided by Financing Activities.

StartUp Step 24: Now that you've had the opportunity to review Sergio's Cash Flow Statement, it's time to create your own cash flow statement based on your business' financial information. If you are just starting your business, you may not have enough financial data needed to generate an accurate cash flow statement. If this applies to you, log on to the StartingUp Skill Center and download sample cash flow statements by industry. This will also help make you aware of the specific Cash Receipts/Cash Paid items you need to add in order to customize your own cash flow statement. This is quite common as you adapt your cash flow statement to your own business or industry. Use the Cash Flow chart above to get started.

KEEP IT GOING

VIEW CASH FLOW STATEMENTS BY INDUSTRY AT WWW.STARTINGUPNOW.COM.

For Year Ending December 31, 2009		
Cash at Beginning of Period		
Operating Activities		
Net Income		
Cash Paid for		
Inventory Purchases		
Operational Expenses		
Salaries		
Net Cash provided by Operating Expenses		
Investing Activities		
Cash Receipts from		
Sale of Equipment or Property		
Sale of Investment Securities		
Cash Paid for		
Purchase of Equipment		
Loans to Others		
Purchase of Investment Securities		
Net Cash Provided by Investment Activities		
Financing Activities		
Cash Receipts from Issuance of Stock		
Cash Receipts from Loans		
Cash Paid for Purchase of Stock		
Cash Paid for Loan Repayments		
Dividends to Investors		
Net Cash Provided by Financing Activities		

Maxim: "If there is no struggle, there is no progress."
—*Frederick Douglass*

STARTINGUP NOW

SOLIDIFY THE PLAN

Now that you've completed each StartingUp Key Lesson, use the following template to culminate your own business plan based on what you've learned. Be sure to incorporate your notes from each StartingUp Step as they will serve to assist with your company's development.

Once you've finished each of these sections, enter your information online at www.startingupnow.com using the "Business Plan Template," and then print your complete business plan for presentation.

The end result will be a succinct but detailed plan designed to move your business idea into the marketplace. Be sure to utilize helpful tips, tools, and resources found at www.startingupnow.com.

STARTING UP NOW

VAL Incorporate your notes from Step 1 to identify and articulate your company's Core Values.

MST Incorporate your notes from Step 2 to identify and articulate your company's Mission Statement.

STARTING UP NOW

VIS Incorporate your notes from Step 3 to identify and articulate your company's Vision Statement. Remember: keep it short.

EXE Incorporate your notes from Step 4 to identify and articulate your company's Executive Summary.

STARTING UP NOW

ESP Incorporate your notes from Step 5 to identify and articulate your company's Elevator Speech.

BIO Incorporate your notes from Step 6 to write your Biography. Tell your story.

STARTING UP NOW

IDEA

Incorporate your notes from Step 7 to identify and articulate your company's Idea.

LEG

Incorporate your notes from Step 8 to identify and articulate your company's Legal Structure.

MGMT

Incorporate your notes from Step 9 to identify and articulate your company's Management Team.

STARTING UP NOW

YOGA

Incorporate your notes from Step 10 to identify and articulate your company's Year One Goals & Activities.

SHORT TERM LONG TERM

MIA

Incorporate your notes from Step 11 to identify and articulate your company's Industry Analysis.

STARTING UP NOW

MKTG

Incorporate your notes from Step 12 to identify and articulate your company's Marketing Strategy.

MARKETING STRATEGY	
People:	
Product:	
Price:	
Place:	
Promotion:	
Presentation:	

STARTING UP NOW

TCP

Incorporate your notes from Step 13 to identify and articulate your company's Target Customer Profile.

STARTING UP NOW

FAB

Incorporate your notes from Step 14 to identify and articulate your company's Features and Benefits.

FEATURES	BENEFITS

SELL

Incorporate your notes from Step 15 to identify and articulate your company's Sales Strategy.

STARTING UP NOW

COMP

Incorporate your notes from Step 16 to identify and articulate your company's Competition. Use the chart found on page 42 as your guide.

Product:	Local Store	National Chain	Specialty Store

S.W.O.T.S.

Incorporate your notes from Step 17 to identify and articulate your company's S.W.O.T.S.

AD

Incorporate your notes from Step 18 to identify and articulate your company's Advertising Message. Don't forget to upload your video as part of your presentation.

SUC

Incorporate your notes from Step 19 to identify and articulate your company's Startup Costs.

Item	Unit Cost	Quantity	Vendor	Discount %	Sub-Total

OPEX

Incorporate your notes from Step 20 to identify and articulate your company's Operational Expenses.

U-tilities	Budgeted Amount
S-alaries	
A-dvertising	
I-nsurance	
I-nterest	
R-ent	
M-iscellaneous	
Total	

COG

Incorporate your notes from Step 21 to identify and articulate your company's Cost of Goods.

INST Incorporate your notes from Step 22 to identify and articulate your company's Income Statement.

Total Revenue			
Sales			
Cost of Goods Sold			
Gross Profit			
Operating Expenses			
Variable Cost (10% of Sales)			
Fixed Costs			
	Utilities		
	Salaries		
	Advertising		
	Insurance		
	Interest		
	Rent		
	Miscellaneous		
Total Operating Expenses			
Profit Less Operating Expenses			
Charitable Contribution (10%)			
Profit Before Income Taxes			
Income Taxes (25%)			
Net Profit			

BAL

Incorporate your notes from Step 23 to identify and articulate your company's Balance Sheet.

	End Period	Beg Period
Assets		
Current Assets		
Checking/Savings		
Accounts Receivable		
Total Inventory Assets		
Total Current Assets		
Fixed Assets		
Equipment		
Computers		
Printers		
Telephones		
Total Fixed Assets		
Total Current & Fixed Assets		
Liabilities & Equity		
Current Liabilities		
Accounts Payable		
Other Current Liabilities		
Total Current Liabilities		
Opening Balance Equity		
Retained Earnings		
Owner's Equity (Company's Net Worth)		
Total Liabilities & Equity		

STARTING UP NOW

CFLOW

Incorporate your notes from Step 24 to identify and articulate your company's Core Values.

For Year Ending		
Cash at Beginning of Period		
Operating Activities		
Net Income		
Cash Paid for		
Inventory Purchases		
Operational Expenses		
Salaries		
Net Cash provided by Operating Expenses		
Investing Activities		
Cash Receipts from		
Sale of Equipment or Property		
Sale of Investment Securities		
Cash Paid for		
Purchase of Equipment		
Loans to Others		
Purchase of Investment Securities		
Net Cash Provided by Investment Activities		
Financing Activities		
Cash Receipts from Issuance of Stock		
Cash Receipts from Loans		
Cash Paid for Purchase of Stock		
Cash Paid for Loan Repayments		
Dividends to Investors		
Net Cash provided by Financing Activities		

STARTING UP NOW

SPECIAL THANKS

Special Thanks to the following persons who have proven to be faithful friends and colleagues. I appreciate your availability, plethora of skills, and often-candid honesty to develop these steps to hopefully serve others who we may never meet.

Lyman C. Howell, MBA

Vicki D. Frye, Brand & Product Developer
Fryeday Everyday

Mark W. Soderquist, Board Member
The Soderquist Family Foundation

STARTING UP NOW

REVIEWERS

Don G. Soderquist, Senior Vice Chairman and Chief Operating Officer
Walmart Stores, Inc.

Raman Chadha, Executive Director & Clinical Professor
DePaul University, Coleman Entrepreneurship Center

Andre Thornton, Sr., Chief Executive Officer
Global Promotions & Incentives, Inc.

Rev. Dr. Hazel A. King, President & Founder
H.A. King & Associates

Jeffrey Weber, MBA, President,
Jeff Weber Ventures, LLC

Dr. Melvin Banks, Sr., Founder
Urban Ministries, Inc.

Dr. Zira J. Smith, Entrepreneurship and Small Business Educator
University of Illinois-Cook County

Pastor Calvin & Tanya Egler, Founders
Passion Ministries

Dr. Andrea Scott, Ph.D., Assistant Professor of Marketing
Graziadio School of Business & Management, Pepperdine University

Harold C. Spooner, Executive Vice-President
Covenant Ministries of Benevolence Covenant Church

Pastor Phil Jackson, Founding Pastor
The House Covenant Church

68428344R00052

Made in the USA
Columbia, SC
09 August 2019